SERVING ON
PROMOTION, TENURE, AND
FACULTY REVIEW COMMITTEES

SERVING ON PROMOTION, TENURE, AND FACULTY REVIEW COMMITTEES

A Faculty Guide

SECOND EDITION

Robert M. Diamond

The National Academy for Academic Leadership

ANKER PUBLISHING COMPANY, INC.
Bolton, Massachusetts

SERVING ON PROMOTION, TENURE, AND
FACULTY REVIEW COMMITTEES
A Faculty Guide

SECOND EDITION

ISBN 1-882982-49-5

Composition by Deerfoot Studios
Cover Design by Deerfoot Studios

Anker Publishing Company, Inc.
176 Ballville Road
P. O. Box 249
Bolton, MA 01740-0249

www.ankerpub.com

About the Author

Robert M. Diamond is Research Professor at Syracuse University, Visiting Professor at the University of South Florida St. Petersburg, and President of the National Academy for Academic Leadership. He was formally Assistant Vice Chancellor, Director of the Center for Instructional Development, and Professor of Instructional Design, Development & Evaluation, and Higher Education at Syracuse University, where he directed the National Project on Institutional Priorities and Faculty Rewards funded by The Carnegie Foundation for the Advancement of Teaching, The Fund for the Improvement of Post Secondary Education, The Lilly Endowment, and The Pew Charitable Trusts. He coauthored the 1987 National Study of Teaching Assistants, the 1992 National Study of Research Universities and the Balance Between Research and Undergraduate Teaching, and was responsible for the design and implementation of Syracuse University's award-winning high school/college transition program, Project Advance. He also codirected the Syracuse University Focus on Teaching Project. Dr. Diamond has published extensively and is a consultant to colleges and universities throughout the world.

TABLE OF CONTENTS

PREFACE

Multiple forces for change are converging at America's colleges and universities—changes that have important implications for faculty roles and conditions of employment. Dramatic increases in enrollment, increasing diversity of student bodies, more competition among institutions and from the private sector, growing demands for institutional accountability, diminishing government support, and increasing availability of technology and associated options for the design and delivery of instruction will all affect institutional priorities and faculty roles.

Employment options for faculty are changing. While we anticipate that some form of tenure will endure for the foreseeable future, an increasing array of options are being presented to those entering the professoriate. The number of part-time faculty continues to increase, as well as the percentage of faculty working on renewable, multiple-year contracts. The nature of faculty work is also changing. Increasingly, faculty are working across traditional disciplinary boundaries and outside the parameters of traditional classroom teaching and publication or funded research. Faculty are working in their communities, in partnerships with school districts and industry, teaching courses online, and developing innovative pedagogies to engage a wider range of learning styles. These new roles call for new thinking about faculty rewards.

New Material

Whether on a tenure track or not, faculty performance will need to be evaluated in a fair and consistent manner. As institutional priorities shift, so must the expectations for faculty work as embodied in the criteria for faculty review and rewards. The new material you will find in this second edition of *Serving on Promotion, Tenure, and Faculty Review Committees* reflects dynamic changes in the academic workplace and addresses some of the problems that surfaced in the 1990s. Greater attention is paid to evaluating interdisciplinary work as well as technology-based teaching and research and the changing roles of faculty. A new section in this edition addresses the importance of assessing faculty collegiality or campus citizenship in ways that ensure fair treatment and safeguard academic freedom. This new edition also contains information on documenting an instructional innovation or use of technology and the narrative portions of the teaching portfolio. Two new examples have been included in the disciplinary statements and a new section on documenting effectiveness and impact as a member of a team has been added. Finally, we have included a characteristics model for describing faculty scholarship that we believe has decided advantages over traditional definitions and approaches.

The purpose of this guide is to make your work easier. Faculty review is a difficult and labor intensive process. Our goal here is to support a review process that is fair to faculty working in a variety of arrangements within your institutional context.

I hope we have succeeded.

Robert M. Diamond
The National Academy for Academic Leadership
October 2001

ACKNOWLEDGMENTS

I would like to thank the following for their excellent suggestions as this second edition was being developed: Bronwyn Adam, John Centra, Carla Howery, Cathy Trower, and Dan Wheeler. I would also like to express my appreciation to the numerous faculty and administrators who provided me with feedback on the first edition as they used it on their campuses. It's always nice to know that something you have written is proving to be useful.

Finally, I would like to thank Patricia St. Clair for her invaluable clerical assistance during the development of this manuscript.

INTRODUCTION

There are essentially four types of faculty review for which committees are formed: tenure, post-tenure, promotion, and in the case of multi-year appointments, contract renewal. While the focus of these committees is somewhat different, the questions that are asked, much of the data that is collected, and the need for a high-quality and equitable process is fairly consistent.

One of the most important roles you will have as a faculty member is serving on one of these committees. You may have been nominated for this position, you may have been selected for this assignment by a vote of the faculty in your department, or you may be serving by virtue of your faculty rank. The decision(s) you and your committee make will have a major impact on the lives of faculty members being reviewed and will have a significant and long-term impact on your department, school, college, and institution. It is your committee's responsibility to ensure that the review process is fair and that it takes into account a wide range of appropriate considerations—no easy task.

Documenting the Process

As you work through the review process, it is important that you document the steps taken, the data collected, and the rationale for your decision. In this period of diminishing institutional resources and reduced faculty mobility, there is an increasing possibility that candidates will appeal or even turn to the courts to reverse a negative decision. It is for these reasons, as well as for reasons of fairness to the faculty member being reviewed, that your committee's deliberations be sensitive to the broad range of factors that determine the role of a faculty member in a specific department at your institution. It is your responsibility to ensure that the final decision is based on sound documentation and is the result of an open discussion among the committee members.

This guide has been designed to assist you and your committee through the review process. By identifying specific issues that you should consider, listing a number of questions that you might ask, and providing suggestions concerning certain types of documentation, the guide can facilitate your discussions and encourage a fair and open review process. This guide may suggest a number of practices that may be precluded by policies and procedures in place at your institution. If this is the case, your committee might want to propose revisions in the promotion and/or tenure process that would address the concerns we have identified. To assist you further, we have included a list of additional resources or references.

There are several other factors to keep in mind as you read these materials. First, in certain contexts the options available to the committee may be limited by existing departmental and institutional policies. Second, whereas in some situations a single promotion, tenure, or faculty review committee will serve the entire campus, at larger institutions there may be as many as three committee layers in the faculty review, promotion, and tenure process: department, school/college, and institution. In this type of system, the school/college and institution-wide committees will review both the material provided by the candidate and the documentation and recommendations developed by the first and/or second committees. There will also be instances where promotion will be combined with tenure or reappointment decisions.

The Increasing Complexity of the Faculty Reward System

You and your colleagues serving on the committee will most likely be faced with a process far more difficult and challenging than those who served on promotion/tenure committees in the late 1990s. As colleges and universities develop fairer systems of faculty rewards, there has been an effort to ensure that the criteria used are appropriate for each faculty member being reviewed. As a result, it is not uncommon to find that the weight given to certain types of activities will vary from individual to individual and from academic unit to academic unit. Many campuses are, for example, moving toward differentiated assignments where faculty members are given different roles based on their particular strengths and interests. There may also be significant differences in work that is presented as scholarly, and as a result, the documentation you receive may vary a great deal. You may also find that over the past several years institutional guidelines have changed and that the faculty member may have the option of selecting the system under which he or she will be judged.

There will also be differences in the scope of your charge based on the nature of the institution in which you work and in the specific type of contract the faculty member you are reviewing works under. There have been an increasing number of faculty on multi-year renewable contracts, and the use of part-time tenure line positions is also expected to increase. Both of these approaches will directly affect the timeline and the criteria used in the review process. In addition, as institutions attempt to move from one Carnegie classification to another, called by some "mission creep," there is a tendency to change tenure criteria and to raise the tenure bar. If you are on such a campus, you can anticipate major modifications in both the documentation that is required and the standards that must be met. The same trend toward raised standards also appears in those institutions where a formal or informal decision has been made to cap the percentage of faculty that can hold tenured positions.

Since the roles of institutional, school/college, and departmental committees vary, not all of the practices suggested in this guide will be appropriate to every situation. In addition, as faculty work becomes increasingly multidisciplinary, your committee must ensure that an appropriate weight is placed on all aspects of the work and that the weight placed on the information from various academic units is appropriate. When you serve on a committee reviewing candidates from other disciplines, there is simply no way for you to acquire the background necessary to evaluate the disciplinary expertise of the faculty member. In these instances you must rely on specialists in the field. Other factors such as the type of institution and its priorities and the specific assignment that a faculty member has will also have an impact on the scope and focus of your review. What is essential is that the information provided to you be of a nature and quality that enables you to make an informed judgment.

Finally, on some campuses there are distinct differences in the criteria applied for promotion and for tenure. In these instances, whereas promotion decisions tend to focus primarily on the candidate's accomplishments to-date, tenure considerations tend to consider carefully the candidate's long-term promise or potential. Such decisions require the ability to project or predict how productive the candidate will be in meeting future needs of the academic unit and institution. There also may be instances where promotion, particularly to full professor, may require a more national or international reputation and more scholarly work. For these reasons, there may be separate committees for promotion, tenure, and contract renewal review.

Using this Manual

To assist you in making use of this guidebook, we have divided it into two parts. Part I focuses on the general process and the role of the promotion, tenure, and faculty review committee. It provides basic principles, raises a number of important issues, introduces a comprehensive approach to documenting and assessing faculty work, and provides several checklists you may find useful.

Part II includes resources selected for their potential value to the committee, such as statements from discipline-based groups, references for teaching evaluation, an excerpt from an instrument used to evaluate advising, and a number of examples that outline how different types of faculty work might be documented and assessed. The guide concludes with a checklist for use by the committee.

You will also note that particular attention has been paid to several areas of faculty work that have become increasing problematic for a number of committees. First, it addresses the question of what scholarly work actually is. This has become a major issue as the scope of scholarly work has expanded and an increasing number of disciplines have enlarged the range of activities that qualify. Second, as more and more faculty work is done as part of a team, you face the question of what exactly the candidate's role was in this activity and his or her contribution. In later pages you will find specific guidelines to assist you in both areas.

The purpose of this guide is to serve as a helpful reference for you, other members of your committee, the individuals who will review your decision, and the candidate under consideration. We hope you find the suggestions to the point, highly applicable, and easy to use.

PART I
PROCESS

SOME BASIC PRINCIPLES

The committee must be sensitive to the disciplinary perspectives of its members.

Each of us brings to any committee on which we serve the vocabulary, traditions, standards, and perceptions of our own discipline. We may not always be aware of the degree to which our values and assumptions affect our judgment of colleagues' work. Attitudes and beliefs become particularly important when we serve on promotion and tenure committees composed of faculty from various fields or when the faculty member being reviewed is from a discipline distinctly different from our own. The scientific paradigm that values traditional research and publication may work fairly well to measure the significance of much of the work in the social and natural sciences, but it may be inappropriate when applied to major areas of faculty work in the humanities, professional schools, and creative arts.

Even when reviewing the work of a faculty member from your own department, there will be times when you may not have the expertise to assess the quality of the work being considered by the committee, and as a result, you may need to turn to others to help provide an assessment. Remember, too, that there is no single determinant of what constitutes quality professional and disciplinary work or scholarship. One of the greatest and most difficult challenges your committee will face is to develop an understanding of scholarly, professional, and creative work in disciplines far different from those represented in the committee membership.

The committee must be sensitive to the impact of technology and the changing roles of faculty.

A number of forces are at work that are having a major impact on the role of faculty, on what they are asked to do, and on the criteria that you will need to use in the assessment process. It can be anticipated that the candidates you review will be extremely diverse not only in their disciplines but in their roles, their strengths, and in the forms that their scholarship may take. The move toward differentiated staffing, where individual faculty are assigned to roles that build on their specific expertise and interests, is becoming more common as institutions attempt to make maximum use of the talents they have available.

An increasing number of institutions will be actively using technology to redesign courses and curricula, develop educational and professional software, and explore new ways to improve learning and deliver instruction. As noted earlier, you can also anticipate an increased involvement in teamwork where the major scholarly initiative of a faculty member may not only include other faculty, often from other disciplines, but specialists in technology, instructional design, or assessment.

As technology becomes more readily available, and as students enter the institution with stronger technological backgrounds, one of the topics you will want to address is how well a faculty member is utilizing these advances in his or her teaching. Do you find evidence of continuing professional development? Is the faculty member learning new skills and exploring new approaches? Do you see examples of the candidate's awareness of new web applications, email, and recent developments in teaching and learning?

You will also find a growing number of instances where the priorities for faculty work will be established, not by the individual, but by his or her academic unit or by the administration of the institution. Faculty may, for example, be asked to participate in instructional projects that expand access and enhance quality while reducing or containing the costs of instruction, produce a technologically based product, or solve other specific institutional problems. As faculty roles become more complex, we can expect that both the committee and the candidate will need to collect supportive data from a far wider group of experts and colleagues than ever before.

The expanding nature of scholarly, professional, and creative work will also place increased pressure on both the candidate and his or her academic unit to provide specific information as to the charge that has been given, what was expected, and the specific role of the individual in team-related initiatives.

The committee must be sensitive to a number of common assumptions about teaching that are not supported by research.

Many myths permeate our perceptions about teaching and research and consequently affect faculty reward traditions in higher education. After reviewing over 2,600 published accounts of the effects of college on students, Terenzini and Pascarella (1994) identify a number of myths about higher education, one of which is particularly germane to our consideration of promotion and tenure review—that "good researchers are good teachers" (p. 30). This assumption, some would say, has underpinned our emphasis in promotion and tenure review on research production rather than teaching effectiveness. Actually, Terenzini and Pascarella note only a small correlation between scholarly production and instructional effectiveness, suggesting that each dimension must be assessed separately because strength in one role does not necessarily indicate strength in the other.

There is also a perception on the part of some faculty that teaching cannot be evaluated. But as we will discuss in more detail later, techniques do exist. The problem of evaluating teaching effectiveness is one of time and resources. In the past, individuals and institutions have been unwilling to devote the resources and energy necessary for such an evaluation. Until an appropriate level of energy is devoted to the task, teaching will never be given the weight it deserves in the faculty evaluation process.

The better the information the candidate receives as he or she prepares for review, the easier the process will be for both the candidate and the committee.

Long before a candidate must submit documentation to the committee, she or he should be provided information in four general areas. The three-year review may be the appropriate time to preview the tenure or review process for new faculty, or it may be the practice at your institution for faculty mentors to assume responsibility for briefing candidates on the following areas.

The type of documentation the committee expects

- If scholarship is a major element of the portfolio, what are the criteria that will be used to determine if an activity meets the stated requirements? What materials should be included for review?

- If a professional or teaching portfolio is expected or encouraged, what should be included, and how should it be organized and presented?

- What specific types of materials regarding the other roles of the faculty member are expected?

- Will the candidate be asked to provide copies of the publications he or she feels are most significant?

- Should the candidate provide letters of support and, if so, from whom and how many?

- Should the candidate provide a list of references, and, if so, when?

- How much material should be presented and on what timeline?

Your committee may be inundated by useless or irrelevant material if you do not articulate clear expectations and guidelines. Information of this type can be developed at the school, college, or department level and ideally should be provided to candidates when they first arrive at the institution.

The specific steps that will be followed by the committee(s)

- What steps will the committee follow, and what is the anticipated timeline? Will the committee interview other faculty?

- Will documentation or assessment be requested from individuals outside of the institution?

- How are these external reviewers going to be selected?

- Do you expect nominations from the candidate?

It is also important that you remind the candidate that colleagues from other disciplines will be reviewing his or her work.

Detailed recommendations to help you in developing a set of resources for candidates are found in the materials that follow.

The criteria that will be used to assess the quality of the materials that are provided

- Publications, for example, can be reviewed in many ways. Will they simply be counted using some formula for weighing, or will a small number be reviewed against a specific set of standards?

- How will the quality of teaching or advising be determined and how will the quality and significance of other professional activities be measured?

How the various activities of the faculty member will be weighed

- Is there a set formula for the importance of specific functions, or will these be determined on an individual basis according to assignment and documentation? It should be noted that as the review process becomes more sensitive to the differing roles of faculty, the attempt to use the same fraction of weight for research, teaching, and service for all faculty becomes increasingly impractical.

- Is there a particular approach for determining weight of the activities?

Other issues that should be addressed

The practical guide *Good Practice in Tenure Evaluation* (2000), a joint project of the American Council on Education, the American Association of University Professors, and United Educators Insurance, highlights several additional areas of importance that should be addressed in your procedural guidelines for any formal faculty review.

- If positive events occur after the candidate has submitted his or her materials and before a decision is made, can they be considered and under what conditions?

- There should also be a plan for handling allegations of misconduct or other negative information that may come to the attention of the committee during the process.

- What weights, if any, will be given to informal and unsolicited opinions, and should the candidate be advised about such information?

- If a senior faculty member serves on both the college-wide and departmental or school committees, does he or she have voting rights on each?

This 30-page publication also includes an excellent section on caring for unsuccessful candidates, a very important but often overlooked element in the tenure, promotion, and review process. A free electronic version of the manual is available through www.acenet.edu/bookstore/.

2

IMPORTANT CONSIDERATIONS

In reviewing the candidacy of each faculty member, it is essential that the committee clearly understands what expectations were in place at the time of the candidate's hire. If criteria have recently changed, which of the standards will be used? As noted earlier, in many institutions this choice is up to the candidate and it is important for the committee to make sure that it, the candidate, and the institution are all playing by the same rules.

Existing Policies and Statements Relating to Promotion and Tenure

Early in the process the committee should review all published policies and procedures relating to the promotion and tenure process. At many institutions these differ significantly from school to school and from program to program. Some institutions publish specific statements regarding criteria that should be met for promotion to the rank of full professor. Because, as noted above, criteria change over time, it is important to be sure that you are using those that apply to the individual candidate.

The Priorities of the Institution

What are the stated missions of the institution, and how do the strengths and work of the faculty member fit with and support these goals?

The Priorities of the Academic Unit

What are the priorities of the academic unit? How important is the work of the candidate to the health and vitality of the department?

How do the individual strengths of the candidate support the long-term growth of the department and meet specific needs that are not otherwise met?

The Differences among the Disciplines

There are major differences among the disciplines, both in terms of faculty practices and methodology and in the language they use to describe their work. These differences can create problems as faculty members come up for review by faculty from other disciplines, particularly if the work presented is not in the form of traditional research and publication. This problem was addressed in a document prepared for the American Historical Association by a committee established to address definitions of scholarship in history.

> The debate over priorities is not discipline-specific but extends across the higher education community. Nevertheless, each discipline has specific concerns and problems. For history, the privilege given to the monograph in promotion and tenure has led to the undervaluing of other activities central to the life of the discipline—writing textbooks, developing courses and curricula, documentary editing, museum exhibitions, and film projects to name but a few. (American Historical Association Ad hoc Committee on Redefining Scholarly Work, 1994)

To provide assistance in the assessment of faculty work, a number of discipline associations have participated in a project centered at Syracuse University (sponsored by The Carnegie Foundation for the Advancement of Teaching, The Fund for the Improvement of Post Secondary Education, The Lilly Endowment, and The Pew Charitable Trusts) to develop comprehensive statements describing the scholarly and professional work in their respective fields. These statements provide valuable insights for those confronting the discipline-specific nature of scholarship. In Part II you will find brief segments from several statements (history, business, theater, mathematics, physics, and psychology). These have been selected to show the differences among the disciplines, and how each is attempting to expand the scope of work that is considered scholarly. The completed statements from over 25 disciplines can be found in a two-volume set, *The Disciplines Speak* (Diamond & Adam, 1996 & 2000), published by the American Association for Higher Education. Included are statements from the following:

Volume I: 1995
> American Academy of Religion
> American Chemical Society
> American Historical Association
> Association for Education in Journalism and Mass
> Communications
> Association of American Geographers
> Association to Advance Collegiate Schools of Business
> Council of Administrators of Family and Consumer Sciences
> Joint Policy Board for Mathematics
> National Office for Arts Accreditation in Higher Education
> Landscape Architectural Accreditation Board
> National Architectural Accrediting Board
> National Association of Schools of Art and Design
> National Association of Schools of Dance
> National Association of Schools of Music
> National Association of Schools of Theatre

Volume II: 2000
> American Association of Colleges for Teacher Education
> American Association of Colleges of Nursing
> American Association of Medical Colleges (Status Report)
> American Physical Society
> American Psychological Association
> American Society of Civil Engineers
> Association of College and Research Libraries
> Council on Social Work Education
> Modern Language Association
> National Council for Black Studies
> National Women's Studies Association
> Society for College Science Teachers

If you are considering a candidate in any of the medical fields, an excellent resource is *Redefining Scholarship in Contemporary Academic Medicine* (Association of American Medical Colleges, 2000).

The Time in a Faculty Member's Career When the Review Is Taking Place

As you review the materials provided to you, it is important to keep in mind that individual priorities, departmental assignments, and the nature of a particular discipline will all affect how a faculty member spends his or her time. In some fields the most creative research a faculty member does is early in a career; in others, many years of study and experience after graduate school will be necessary before a significant scholarly contribution can be expected. There are also instances where faculty members, based on earlier work or changing interests, may move in a significantly different direction in their scholarly or professional work than was originally intended. There is no single yardstick for success.

New and Developing Disciplines

If your candidate is from one of the newer disciplines (for example, bioengineering, robotics, or entrepreneurism), both the committee and the faculty member face distinct challenges. In new fields a research history or tradition will not exist, and publication outlets may not have been established. In addition, much of the work may appear in very nontraditional forms such as audio histories or in what once were considered underground publications. In new fields, both textbooks and pedagogical methodologies may need to be developed. Scholars in developing fields may have different visions of what should be taught in the first place. As a committee, it will be your responsibility to determine the quality and significance of the work from these nontraditional documentation sources. What is important is that the candidate not be penalized because of the newness of the field or the unfamiliarity of the work to you.

Interdisciplinary or Collaborative Work

One of the more complex challenges you will face is determining both the role and the contributions of a faculty member when he or she is part of a team composed of other faculty, staff, or, in some instances, individuals from outside of the institution. These projects might be research oriented, might focus on teaching-related initiatives, or be in the context of community or organizational service. Your role as a committee will become even more difficult when this activity is being presented by the candidate as his or her scholarly activity.

To collect the necessary information, you must focus on a number of key questions that will need to be asked of both the candidate and other team members. In an effort to collect quality information, a number of questions should focus on the same issues.

Information to be provided by the candidate

- What specific expertise did he or she bring to the project? To be considered scholarly, the candidate's involvement must be in his or her discipline.

- What was the candidate's specific role on the team? Were there certain elements of the project or initiative where he or she had a greater role?

- Were there certain products that were developed for which the candidate played a major role? What were they, how was their effect measured, and what were the results?

- What was the significance of the effort? What impact does it or will it have?

- If this initiative is to be used to meet the scholarship requirement, are all the needed characteristics being met?

Information to be provided by other team members

- What was the role of the candidate on the team?

- Did the candidate bring to the project needed expertise in certain areas? If so, what were they?

- Was the candidate an active and contributing member of the team? Did he or she work effectively with other team members? Were deadlines met and responsibilities fulfilled?

- What were his or her major contributions to the effort?

- From your perspective, what was the significance of the effort and its potential impact?

- In the future, would you choose to work with the candidate on other projects?

In Chapter Nine you will find guidelines that can be provided to help the candidate prepare his or her documentation.

Collegiality

While often difficult to measure by any simple technique, how well a faculty member works with his or her colleagues and within the institution must be a factor considered by the committee. Since a tenure or multi-year decision results in a long-term appointment, how effectively a faculty member contributes to the health of his or her department, or to the institution at large, can be of major importance in the decision-making process. It is, therefore, recommended that the collegiality factor be included in all policy statements. It is important that the focus be on how well a faculty member works with his or her colleagues and how willing he or she is to contribute to meeting the needs of the institution. For legal reasons, the focus should not be on what is said or on the stands that an individual takes, but on the process itself and the willingness of an individual to function in a positive manner as part of the group. An institution must have a way of terminating individuals who are disruptive and counter-productive. It is a fine line between disagreement and destructive behavior, but such a line must exist in the faculty reward system.

A faculty survey instrument that your committee can use to collect information in this area can be found in Chapter Ten. For an excellent review of the arguments for and against considerations of collegiality and a review of relevant case law, see Connell and Savage (2001).

Special Assignments

Most institutions with tenure try to avoid giving new faculty in tenure-line positions specific assignments that may constrain their ability to devote time to the more traditional activities of research and publication. There are instances, however, in which both new and experienced faculty are asked or even required to participate in special projects. Serving on these projects will affect the nature of the documentation the candidate provides to the committee. Special assignments might include serving as department chair, the development of new courses or programs, the development of reports for accreditation or certification, or an administrative assignment that is essential to the health of the department. In a number of cases these activities may be viewed as meeting the necessary criteria to be considered as scholarly in the review process.

Increasingly, the appointment itself specifies a particular set of criteria. For example, in the following advertisement, the University of Kentucky outlines a tenure-track position that is primarily focused on interdisciplinary teaching. Notice how the criteria for tenure are described in the advertisement for the position.

> The University of Kentucky. Department of Geography. ASSISTANT PROFESSOR. Special tenure-track teaching position beginning August 1994. Ph.D. required. The University of Kentucky and the College of Arts & Sciences have recently implemented new initiatives to enhance undergraduate education, including innovative Mini-colleges which offer the opportunity for creative interdisciplinary teaching in smaller class settings, and Special Title teaching appointments such as this one. The primary assignment for this position is to teach four undergraduate courses per semester with occasional graduate level teaching possible. The person hired for this position will also have the opportunity to develop new introductory courses and conduct teaching practicums for graduate instructors. Exceptional teaching skills required. Evaluation and retention will be based upon teaching effectiveness.

To ensure fairness to the faculty member and to the committee, in cases such as the one above it is important that the promotion and tenure criteria are clearly understood, clearly documented, and forwarded to the promotion and tenure committee before the assignment is made. Unfortunately, there will be times when this has not been done, and responsibility will fall to the committee to trace and document the history of the assignment before a promotion, tenure, or contract renewal decision can be fairly made.

Getting the Information

As noted, there will be times when the candidate will provide most of the needed information to you. This is particularly true when an attempt has been made to provide the candidate with clear guidelines on exactly what is required. However, in most instances it will be the responsibility of the committee to obtain those materials that, while needed for their deliberation, have been omitted or overlooked. The following checklist will assist you in this process. Note that in a number of areas you will want to have on hand copies of those policy and procedural statements that were in place when the candidate was hired and those that are now in effect.

If tenure and promotion polices and procedures or institutional, school, college, or departmental missions or priorities have changed between the time a candidate has been hired and when you are conducting your review, it is imperative that your committee review the specific changes that have occurred. When policies have changed, also check to see what provisions have been included to protect the faculty member.

A Checklist of Useful Documents

Institutional

☐ Institutional mission and vision statement when the candidate was hired

☐ Institutional mission and vision statement now in effect

☐ Promotion and tenure guidelines when hired

☐ Promotion and tenure guidelines now in effect

School/College and Department

☐ Mission and vision statement when candidate was hired

☐ Mission and vision statement now in effect

☐ Promotion and tenure guidelines when hired

☐ Promotion and tenure guidelines now in effect

☐ Description of scholarly, professional, or creative work in the discipline

Candidate Specific

☐ Letter of appointment

☐ Formal changes in appointment

☐ Documents of specific assignments or changes in priorities of work

☐ Job description

3

DOCUMENTING AND ASSESSING FACULTY WORK

The promotion and tenure review has three basic parts: 1) the documentation the faculty member provides, 2) the materials the committee collects, and 3) the review of this material by the committee. A well-prepared faculty member can go a long way in making his or her case by providing a strong context and solid documentary materials for the committee to consider.

Many descriptions of the work of faculty have been suggested as alternatives to the traditional three-part model of teaching, research, and service. One expanded taxonomy identifies the following as common discipline-based faculty activities (Gray, Adam, Froh, & Yonai, 1994).

Working with students in many different settings and using many different methods for:

- Teaching undergraduates and graduates
- Advising pre-freshmen to post-doctoral fellows

Citizenship (non-disciplinary):

- Serving on departmental, school, or institutional committees
- Assuming leadership roles within the institution and in professional organizations
- Representing the institution on external committees, task forces, commissions, etc.

Scholarly activity involving:

- Research that leads to the production of intellectual and/or creative works
- Writing for publication, presentation, or performance

Professional service through the application of:

- Disciplinary expertise to assist the institution, citizen groups, government agencies, businesses, industry

Depending on the particular activities the faculty member presents for review, it will be your committee's responsibility to determine both the significance and quality of the work. While the documentation of research and publication has become fairly standardized since the 1980s, demonstration of quality work in other domains is just beginning to receive attention.

What Scholarship Is

In 1990, building on the work of Eugene Rice, Ernest Boyer in *Scholarship Reconsidered* proposed that colleges and universities move beyond the debate of teaching versus research and that the definition of scholarship be expanded to include:

- The scholarship of discovery: original research
- The scholarship of integration: the synthesizing and reintegration of knowledge
- The scholarship of application: professional practice
- The scholarship of teaching: the transformation of knowledge through teaching

This book was to have a profound impact on American higher education. While many institutions and disciplinary associations have used this model as the basis for their expanded approach to describing scholarship, others have modified the four classifications or included them within their own, often traditional, framework. If you are finding these terms in use at your institution and in the policies you are working with, a brief review of *Scholarship Reconsidered* might prove most helpful.

Documenting Scholarly, Professional, and Creative Work

Recognizing that the academy needs a way of describing the scholarly aspects of faculty work that communicates across disciplines, between programs and departments, and among institutions, we need to focus on the common characteristics of scholarly processes and their outcomes.

To do this we build on two earlier publications. The first, *Recognizing Faculty Work* (Diamond & Adam, 1993), developed from the work of their disciplinary associations, identified six characteristics which seemed to typify scholarly processes and production.

- The activity requires a high level of discipline-related expertise.

- The activity breaks new ground or is innovative.

- The activity can be replicated or elaborated.

- The work and its results can be documented.

- The work and its results can be peer reviewed.

- The activity has significance or impact.

In the second, Charles E. Glassick, Mary Taylor Huber, and Gene I. Maeroff build on the earlier work of Ernest Boyer and Eugene Rice and suggest in *Scholarship Assessed* (1997) that six qualitative standards can be applied to scholarly work.

- Clear goals

- Adequate preparation

- Appropriate methods

- Significant results

- Effective presentation

- Reflective critique

While our work with the disciplinary association task forces led us to describe features of the *products* of scholarly, professional, or creative work, Glassick, Huber, and Maeroff's approach focused more on the *process* of scholarship. It is, we believe, a combination of these two aspects—product and process—that will provide us with a practical and functional way of describing and evaluating the scholarly work of faculty. This approach has a number of advantages.

- Individual academic units can be given the responsibility of determining if a specific activity falls within the work of the discipline and the priorities of the institution, school, college, and department.

- The criteria that are used can be relatively clear, easy to understand, and consistent across all disciplines.

- The system is fair and recognizes difference; no one discipline or group of disciplines determining what scholarship should be for another.

- The process is cost-effective. Faculty preparing for review know what is expected of them and the documentation that is required. Faculty serving on review committees can focus on the quality of the product and process and not on whether or not the activity should be considered scholarly.

- This approach can be incorporated easily into the descriptions of scholarly work developed by Boyer and Rice and the more recent work of Hutchings and Shulman (1999).

In addition, this approach eliminates the need to categorize the activity. While what a faculty member does may represent basic or applied research, be in the context of teaching or service or in the creative arts, the setting is not of prime importance. What is important is that the process that is followed and the resultant outcome represent a level of quality supported by appropriate documentation. While it may not be your option as a committee to use this structure, you may have the ability to place it on the agenda of those who are involved in developing procedures and policies at the unit or institutional level.

As noted, it is the role of the academic unit or department to identify those specific areas of work that fall within the priorities of the department, within the context of the discipline, and the mission and vision of the institution. Ideally you, as a committee, should not be placed in a position of having to determine if a specific body of work is appropriate to be considered scholarly. It is, however, your responsibility to determine if the specific criteria for scholarly work was met and fully documented.

TABLE 3.1

An activity will be considered scholarly if it meets the following criteria.

1) The activity or work requires a high level of discipline-related expertise.

2) The activity or work is conducted in a scholarly manner with:

   - Clear goals

   - Adequate preparation

   - Appropriate methodology

3) The activity or work and its results are appropriately documented and disseminated. This reporting should include a reflective component that addresses the significance of the work, the process that was followed, and the outcomes of the research, inquiry, or activity.

4) The activity or work has significance beyond the individual context:

   - Breaks new ground or is innovative

   - Can be replicated or elaborated

5) The activity or work, both process and product or result, is reviewed and judged to be meritorious and significant by a panel of one's peers.

It will be the responsibility of the academic unit to determine if the activity or work falls within the priorities of the department, school/college, discipline, and institution.

While it will be the responsibility of the candidate to provide substantiation of the significance and quality of such work, it is suggested that the committee assist by providing examples or models to follow. This is particularly important if the activity is one that falls outside of traditional areas of research and publication.

Some institutions have published statements or guides that help to substantiate activities that are of particular importance in light of institutional missions. For example, the Office of Continuing Education and Public Service at the University of Illinois at Urbana-Champaign has published *A Faculty Guide for Relating Public Service to the Promotion and Tenure Review Process* (1993).[1] Materials of this type that discuss criteria, documentation, and evaluation in the context of the specific values of the institution can be extremely helpful to both faculty members preparing for review and to the members of the review committee.

DOCUMENTING TEACHING EFFECTIVENESS

In the evaluation of teaching, three basic questions must be addressed:

1) Which characteristics will be evaluated?

2) How will data be collected?

3) Who will do the evaluation?

A number of options exist under each question (see Table 3.2). Evaluation of teaching has depended primarily on student ratings. Such measures, while useful, provide only one vision of teacher effectiveness. The committee should keep in mind that student evaluations are usually collected near the end of the term when many of the failing or unhappy students are no longer in attendance or when those who have remained in class are anxious about final grades. It is interesting to note that few faculty are asked to include in their documentation evidence of student learning.

You should also keep in mind, as is true with service, that teaching can indeed be scholarship and that as Hutchings and Shulman (1999) have so clearly pointed out, there is a distinct difference between the scholarship of teaching and scholarly teaching. Teaching becomes scholarship when it is made public, is available for peer review and critique according to accepted standards, and can be reproduced and built on by other scholars.

In particular disciplines, outcomes of instruction may be easier to demonstrate than in others. In general, the dynamic nature of learning makes documentation complicated. Nonetheless, every attempt should be made to focus on ways in which student learning can be substantiated and documented as part of faculty review. Shifts away from what students say about the teacher and course and toward what students are able to demonstrate as a result of their experience in the course are concomitant with shifts in modes of instruction.

TABLE 3.2

Planning for Evaluating Teaching

Which characteristics will be evaluated?
- Knowledge and uses of the research on teaching and learning
- Clearly stated learning outcomes with appropriate assessment procedures
- Effective and appropriate use of technology
- Appropriate mix of alternative learning strategies
- Good organization of subject matter and course
- Effective communication
- Knowledge of and enthusiasm for the subject matter and teaching
- Positive attitudes toward students
- Fairness in assessment and grading
- Flexibility in approaches to teaching

How will data be collected?
- Self-assessment/report
- Classroom observation
- Structured interview
- Instructional rating survey
- Test or appraisal of student achievement and attitudes
- Content analysis of instructional materials and student manuals
- Review of classroom records
- Alumni survey

Who will do the evaluating?
- Self
- Students
- Faculty
- Dean or department chair
- Alumni
- Other appropriate administrators
- Others participating in class-related activities
- Work or internship supervisor

Modified from: Centra, J., Froh, R. C., Gray, P. J., & Lambert, L. M. (1987). R. M. Diamond (Ed.). *A guide to evaluating teaching for promotion and tenure.* Acton, MA: Copley.

Different measures are appropriate to different student/teacher interactions. Anyone reviewing teaching needs to be sensitive to the fact that many of our standard practices for evaluating teaching are based on traditional models of instruction as well as particular assumptions about the role of teacher that contemporary theories call into question. The role of teacher as lecturer and deliverer of knowledge is an anachronism in many institutions or contexts. As the nature of teaching shifts, and as technology becomes more available, the data that will substantiate or document teaching must shift as well. Our perceptions about the role of teacher and the nature of the learning enterprise must be open to appreciate new roles of faculty members as coaches, facilitators, and co-learners. It will be your responsibility to select that combination of measures that is most appropriate to the teaching of each candidate. References focused on evaluating teaching and the use of the teaching portfolio can be found in Chapter Seven.

DOCUMENTING ADVISING EFFECTIVENESS

While the weight given to advising effectiveness may vary considerably from case to case, it is a common category of faculty work. A number of survey instruments have been developed for this purpose, and as with any instrument of this type, it is advisable that it be used over time so that the faculty member can benefit from the information as part of formative evaluation. For summative purposes, this information can provide documentation to the committee of development in particular areas. One segment of a student survey on academic advising, available through the American College Testing Program (ACT), can be found in Chapter Eight. In addition to the written survey, interviews with a sample of the candidate's advisees can prove to be most informative.

DOCUMENTING NON-DISCIPLINARY SERVICE

While many faculty activities fall under the category of citizenship, the focus of the evaluation must be on the importance of the activities and the quality of the work being performed. The weight given to these activities may vary considerably based on the faculty assignment, the significance of the activity, and the relative weight customarily given to this type of work in promotion and tenure cases on your campus.

THE PROFESSIONAL PORTFOLIO

Documentation of any faculty work should stress two dimensions: 1) the quality of the work, and 2) the significance of the work. In many instances, faculty provide promotion and tenure committees with detailed information as to the quality and quantity of their effort; however, they do not present a case for the value of their work, describing its impact or explaining in what ways and for whom this work has significance.

This information can be collected from a number of sources. What is important is that the material be focused and manageable. For this reason, we encourage a selected professional portfolio in which a selection of materials is reviewed in-depth. Faculty should be advised to be reasonable when they select the number of documents, texts, or artifacts they present in their portfolios, choosing those materials that they feel are most significant and representative. At the same time, promotion and tenure committees should be prepared for the amount of time required to review a portfolio collection of evidence. If several candidates are being reviewed, some have suggested that the committee divide responsibility, with each member reading a few portfolios and each portfolio being read and reported on by a minimum of three members.

A growing number of institutions provide their faculty with specific guidelines to use as they develop their teaching or professional portfolio. The Center for Teaching Excellence at Texas A & M University, The Center for Teaching Excellence at The Ohio State University, and The Center for Effective Teaching and Learning at the University of Texas, El Paso, all have developed guidelines on developing teaching portfolios that you might find useful. The Teaching and Learning Center at the University of Nebraska, Lincoln, has devoted a section of its resource library to this subject and, like a number of other centers, has staff that will assist faculty in the collection of data and portfolio development. Your guidelines to candidates should encourage them to take advantage of the services and resources of the faculty support center office on their campus as they prepare their documentation.

One of the most widely used references on teaching portfolios is Peter Seldin's *The Teaching Portfolio* (1997). In Chapter Thirteen you will find a worksheet based on this reference that a faculty member can use in preparing the narrative portions of his or her portfolio. A list of potential sources of documentation can be found in Table 3.3.

TABLE 3.3

Sources of Documentation (Some Examples)

Establishing Quality

- Expert testimony (formal reviews, juries, and solicited testimony)
- Faculty essay (describing the process that was followed, the rationale behind the decisions that were made, and the quality of the products)
- Formal reports and studies
- Publication, display, or presentation (video based)

Establishing Significance

- Faculty essay (explaining why the work is important, to whom, and for what purposes)
- External reviews focusing on the significance and usefulness of the activity or product
- Impact on the intended audience
  - ~ size and scope
  - ~ documentation (changes in learning, attitudes, performance)
- Relation to the mission statement of the institution/ department
- Documentation of individual assignment (what is the department requiring of the faculty member?)
- Disciplinary statement reinforcing type of work involved
- Initiatives by others that built on this work or applied what has been learned

THE FACULTY ESSAY

As noted in Table 3.3, one excellent source of information is a statement prepared by the faculty member. While this descriptive essay may have a number of functions, its primary purpose is to provide a frame of reference or context for the items submitted to the committee for review. It describes what the faculty member sees as his or her priorities. Most importantly, the descriptive essay provides important information to the committee that would not otherwise be available, such as:

- A description of issues from the faculty member's perspective

- Rationale for choices the faculty member made

- The extent to which the candidate's expectations were met

- Circumstances that promoted or inhibited success

- The significance of this work as an intellectual contribution, from the faculty member's perspective

This document can serve as the basis for the specific questions that are asked of external reviewers, thus focusing their attention on the issues the committee feels are most important. The essay can also be used as a descriptive document that provides a rationale for the materials that have been forwarded to the committee and is one way for the candidate to demonstrate a capacity to be reflective and self-critical, and hence, capable of continued growth and change. The essay also provides the candidate with the opportunity of placing all of his or her work into a single context and of helping the committee focus on what the candidate feels is most important.

It is crucial, however, to remember the distinction between the descriptive essay and the work itself. Faculty members should be judged on the quality of their work. The descriptive essay enhances reviewers' understanding of the work, but does not replace it or its documentation.

EXAMPLES OF DOCUMENTATION

As part of the national Institutional Priorities and Faculty Rewards project coordinated at Syracuse University, faculty teams from several campuses and a range of disciplines considered a number of difficult documentation cases and suggested ways in which specific activities might be documented for a promotion and tenure committee. Several such examples can be found in Chapter Eleven. As you review these examples, please keep in mind that they are illustrative and not intended to be prescriptive in their detail.

Helping to Develop School, College, or Departmental Guidelines

If your committee is given the responsibility to help develop guidelines, there are several useful resources, in addition to those discussed earlier, that will prove most helpful and simplify your task.

In *Aligning Faculty Rewards with Institutional Mission* (Diamond, 1999) you will find detailed suggestions as to what should be included as well as statements, policies, and guidelines from institutions across the country.

Good Practice in Tenure Evaluation (American Council on Education, American Association of University Professors, and United Educators Insurance, 2000) discusses issues that should be addressed and the characteristics of a quality review process. This practical guide also includes several excellent checklists.

Based on a study of 217 institutions, *Policies on Faculty Appointment* (Trower, 2000) reviews how key faculty appointment issues are addressed at a wide range of colleges and universities.

As mentioned previously, a description of the characteristics of scholarly work should be included in all statements.

End Note

[1]Single copies of *A Faculty Guide for Relating Public Service to the Promotion and Tenure Review Process* (1993) are available at no charge by writing to the Office of Continuing Education and Public Service, University of Illinois, 302 E. John Street, Suite 202, Champaign, IL 61820.

4

IN SUMMARY

The work you and your colleagues will do over the next several months as you serve on the promotion, tenure, and faculty review committee is extremely important. Your decision will affect the lives of the faculty you are reviewing and will help determine the future direction of the academic unit you represent. The key to a good decision lies in the process you follow. The better your data and the more open your deliberations, the fairer your decision will be. In Chapter Fourteen you can find a review of the major issues outlined in this guide.

Serving on a promotion, tenure, and faculty review committee is not an easy task. It is difficult, challenging work. It can, however, be a most positive and rewarding professional and personal experience.

References

American Council on Education, American Association of University Professors, & United Educators Insurance. (2000). *Good practice in tenure evaluation: Advice for tenured faculty, department chairs, and academic administrators.* Washington, DC: American Council on Education.

American Historical Association Ad hoc Committee on Redefining Scholarly Work. (1994). *Redefining historical scholarship.* Washington, DC: American Historical Association.

Association of American Medical Colleges. (2000). *Redefining scholarship in contemporary academic medicine: Essays on scholarship sponsored by the AAMC Council of Academic Societies.* Washington, DC: Author.

Boyer, E. (1990). *Scholarship reconsidered: Priorities of the professoriate.* Princeton, NJ: The Carnegie Foundation for the Advancement of Teaching.

Centra, J., Froh, R. C., Gray, P. J., & Lambert, L. M. (1987). R. M. Diamond (Ed.). *A guide to evaluating teaching for promotion and tenure.* Acton, MA: Copley.

Connell, M. A., & Savage, F. (2001, Spring). The role of collegiality in higher education tenure, promotion, and termination decisions. *Journal of College and University Law, 27* (4), 833–859.

Diamond, R. M., & Adam, B. E. (1993). *Recognizing faculty work: Reward systems for the year 2000.* New Directions in Higher Education, No. 81. San Francisco, CA: Jossey-Bass.

Diamond, R. M., & Adam, B. E. (1996 & 2000). *The disciplines speak* (Vols. 1–2). Washington, DC: The National Association for Higher Education.

Glassick, C. E., Huber, M. T., & Maeroff, G. I. (1997). *Scholarship assessed: Evaluation of the professorate.* San Francisco, CA: Jossey-Bass.

Gray, P. J., Adam, B. E., Froh, R., & Yonai, B. (1994). *Defining, assigning, and assessing faculty work.* New Directions in Institutional Research, No. 84. San Francisco, CA: Jossey-Bass.

Hutchings, P., & Shulman, L. S. (1999, September/October). The scholarship of teaching: New elaborations, new developments. *Change,* 11–15.

Office of Continuing Education and Public Service. (1993). *A faculty guide for relating public service to the promotion and tenure review process.* Champaign, IL: University of Illinois at Urbana-Champaign.

Terenzini, P. A., & Pascarella, E. T. (1994, January/February). Living with myths: Undergraduate education in America. *Change,* 28–32.

Trower, C. A. (2000). *Policies on faculty appointment: Standard practices and unusual arrangements.* Bolton, MA: Anker.

PART II
RESOURCES

5

THE DISCIPLINES CONSIDER SCHOLARSHIP

As noted previously, over 25 scholarly and professional associations have, as part of a project at Syracuse University funded by The Carnegie Foundation for the Advancement of Teaching, The Fund for the Improvement of Post Secondary Education, The Lilly Endowment, and The Pew Charitable Trusts, developed statements that describe the scholarly, professional, and creative work of faculty in their disciplines. Published and distributed by the associations, these statements in their entirety have been published in a two-volume set, *The Disciplines Speak* (Diamond & Adam, 1996 & 2000), by the American Association for Higher Education.

The following examples from these statements display the wide range of faculty work and how different the disciplines are from one another, not only in what faculty do but in how scholarship is described.

Example 1

From the American Historical Association Report, *December 1993*

Adopting the Rice formulation of scholarship, the committee proposes that:

1) **The advancement of knowledge includes:**

   - Original research—based on manuscript and printed sources, material culture, oral history interviews, or other source materials—published in the form of a monograph or refereed journal article; or disseminated through a paper or lecture given at a meeting or conference or through a museum exhibition or other project or program; or presented in a contract research report, policy paper, or other commissioned study

   - Documentary or critical editions

   - Translations

2) **The integration of knowledge includes:**

   - Synthesis of scholarship—published in a review essay (journal or anthology), textbook, newsletter, popular history, magazine, encyclopedia, newspaper, or other form of publication; disseminated through a paper or lecture given at a meeting or conference or through a museum exhibition, film, or other public program; or presented in a contract research report, policy paper, or other commissioned study

   - Edited anthologies, journals, or series of volumes comprised of the work of other scholars

3) **The application of knowledge includes:**

   - Public history, specifically:

Public programming (exhibitions, tours, etc.) in museums and other cultural and educational institutions

Consulting and providing expert testimony on public policy and other matters

Contract research on policy formation and policy outcomes

Participation in film and other media projects

Writing and compiling institutional and other histories

Historic preservation and cultural resource management

Administration and management of historical organizations and institutions

Archival administration and the creation of bibliographies and databases

Professional services—editing journals and newsletters, organizing scholarly meetings, etc.

Community service drawing directly upon scholarship—through state humanities councils (e.g., public lectures), history day competitions, etc.

4) The transformation of knowledge through teaching includes:

- Student mentoring/advising

- Research, writing, and consulting in history education and in other disciplines allied to history

- Development of courses, curricula, visual materials, and teaching materials (including edited anthologies, textbooks, and software)—implemented in the classroom or disseminated through publications (books, professional newsletter articles, etc.), papers (annual meetings, teaching conferences, etc.), or non-print forms

- Organization and participation in collaborative content-based programs (workshops, seminars, etc.) with the schools

- Participation in developing and evaluating advanced placement and other forms of assessment

- Museum exhibitions, catalogs, film, radio, etc.—public programs as forms of teaching

Example 2

The Association to Advance Collegiate Schools of Business (Formerly, The American Assembly of Collegiate Schools of Business), *June 1992*

- **Basic scholarship: The creation of new knowledge**
  Outputs from basic scholarship activities include publication and refereed journals, research monographs, scholarly books, chapters in scholarly books, proceedings from scholarly meetings, papers presented at academic meetings, publicly available research working papers, and papers presented at faculty research seminars. Discovery research, the testing of theories, is included along with developing theories based on case development. Interdisciplinary work across fields, e.g., environmental studies and management, or language studies and international business, are also included.

- **Applied scholarship: The application, transfer, and interpretation of knowledge to approved management practice and teaching**
  Outputs from applied/service scholarship activities include publication and professional journals, professional presentations, public/trade/practitioner journals, in-house book reviews, and papers presented at faculty workshops. Also included are case writing to illustrate existing theories, adapting pure research of others into text, service to community (e.g., internships and case enrichment), interpreting real world experience to classroom use that is generalizable and reusable, and interdisciplinary work across fields such as environmental studies in management or language studies and international business.

- **Instructional development: The enhancement of the educational value of instructional efforts of the institution or discipline**
  Outputs from instructional development activities include textbooks, publications and pedagogical journals, written cases with instructional materials, instructional software, and publicly available materials describing the design and implementation of new courses. Also included are executive education course teaching,

internships supervised by faculty, and materials used to enhance student learning, e.g., for advising and mentoring students and for assessment. In addition, developing new curriculum materials or support materials to be used by others (slides, video presentations, computer software, teachers' manuals) are included.

Example 3

From *The Work of the Theater Faculty*, from the National Office for Arts Accreditation in Higher Education, 1993

CREATIVE WORK AND RESEARCH

Creating Theater

- Creating a work of theater: study, research, and synthesis that lead to original works; translations, interpretations, and adaptations (full-length and one-act plays, screenplays, children's theater); contribution and participation as a collaborative artist in the creation of theater

- Performing a work of theater: study, research, and practice that lead to live or broadcast performance, films or videos, including acting; directing; stage, costume, and lighting designing; technical directing; dramaturgy

Studying Theater and its Influences

- Analyzing how works of theater function: dramatic theory, criticism, interpretation

- Investigating and understanding the history and impact of theater: repertory; studies and analyses from historical, geographical, cultural, and other perspectives; history of ideas in theater; performance practices; bibliography; textual criticism and editing

- Researching the physiological and psychological impact of theater: perceptions of theatrical phenomena; relationship of theater to various specialized audiences; therapeutic applications

- Exploring the sociological impact of theater: theater and the human condition; theater and society; ethnographic and demographic studies; marketing

- Creating and assessing ideas and values about theater: aesthetics, criticism, and philosophy of theater

- Theater design and engineering

- Considering the multiple influences on theater from various sources: conditions, events, ideas, and technologies
- Integrating and synthesizing some or all of the above

Advancing the Pedagogy of Theater

- Developing instructional materials, curricula, and technologies that have broad impact on the field
- Determining causes and effects in education settings
- Integrating and applying theoretical and practical knowledge in educational policy settings
- Exploring philosophical, sociological, and historical connections between theater and education

Applying Theater and Facilitating Theater Activities

- Exploring and developing connections between theater and such areas as administration, commerce, public relations, therapies, and technologies; administration of presenting organizations and venues; artist and repertory management; theater-related industries; copyright; media arts
- Developing and practicing drama therapy
- Programming and publishing works of theater: designing or serving as artistic director of festivals; summer programs; theater series; workshops; master classes; seminars
- Exhibiting, programming, and publishing explanations, studies, and critiques; research and scholarly findings; translations and compilations; books and chapters in books, articles, monographs; delivering or publishing conference papers, panel discussions, proceedings; lectures; reviews of books, performances, productions, or new works of theater; appointments as artist-in-residence; performances as part of professional meetings; workshops; master classes, interviews; seminars; computer applications; program notes; exhibitions of stage and historical costume, stage designs, etc.

Example 4

From the Joint Policy Board for Mathematics Report, *1994*

Defining Mathematical Scholarship

College and university faculty members are scholars as well as teachers. They must stay abreast of the latest developments in their fields in order to remain effective as teachers. Society looks to academia to advance the frontiers of knowledge and to communicate those advances not only to their students, but also to the larger public. Colleges and universities provide a particularly supportive environment for free inquiry, discovery, and the incubation of ideas. Academic scholars provide an important resource that can be drawn upon to address pressing local, regional, and national needs.

But what is scholarship? For some, scholarship is defined narrowly as research leading to new knowledge that is publishable in the leading research journals. Others define scholarship broadly as any activity that leads to increased knowledge or understanding on the part of the individual scholar. Between these two extremes is a variety of activities that may or may not be recognized as scholarly by those who make judgments about scholarship: deans, department chairs, colleagues and students, journal editors, and the public.

Each mathematical sciences department should formulate an explicit and public definition of scholarship that will inform its faculty members about the kinds of scholarly activity that are valued by the department, guide administrators and review committees that are charged with evaluating and rewarding that scholarship, and help all interested parties to understand the scholarly component of the departmental mission. This definition should, of course, be consistent with the mission of the institution. It should embrace the variety of scholarly activities in all fields that the institution and the department wish to encourage and support.

Following is a draft definition of scholarship for the mathematical sciences that may serve as a guide to departments seeking to formulate their own definitions. This draft will, of course, need to be modified by each department to reflect its own values and mission and to conform to the institutional mission.

Scholarship in the mathematical sciences includes:

- Research in core or applied areas that leads to new concepts, insights, discoveries, structures, theorems, or conjectures

- Research that leads to the development of new mathematical techniques, or new applications of known techniques, for addressing problems in other fields including the sciences, social sciences, medicine, and engineering

- Research in teaching and learning that leads to new insights into how mathematical knowledge and skills are most effectively taught and learned at all levels

- Synthesis, or integration, of existing scholarship, such as surveys, book reviews, and lists of open problems

- Exposition that communicates mathematics to new audiences, or to established audiences with improved clarity, either orally or in writing, including technical communications to scientists, engineers, and other mathematicians, as well as books, articles, multimedia materials and presentations for teachers, government leaders, and the general public

- Development of courses, curricula, or instructional materials for teaching mathematics in K–12 as well as at the college level

- Development of software that provides new or improved tools for supporting research in mathematics or its applications, for communicating mathematics, or for teaching and learning mathematics

Good scholarship, in whatever form it takes, must be shared in order to have value. It must benefit more than just the scholar. The results of scholarly activities must be public and must be amenable to evaluation. Techniques appropriate for the evaluation of scholarship in the mathematical sciences include peer review and invitations to present results to others; awards and other forms of recognition; and impact measure, such as citations, evidence of the use of scholarship in the work of others; evidence of improved effectiveness of a technique or activity as a result of the scholarly contribution; or evidence of improved effectiveness of a technique or activity as a result of the scholarly contribution; or evidence of improved understanding of mathematics on the part of some consumer groups as a result of the scholarly activity.

[Reprinted from the Joint Policy Board for Mathematics report, *Recognition and Rewards in the Mathematical Sciences,* with permission of the American Mathematical Society.]

Example 5

From *Faculty Rewards and Recognition in Physics*

A REPORT FROM THE TASK FORCE ON FACULTY REWARDS AND
RECOGNITION COMMITTEE ON EDUCATION (1998)

There is need to reexamine the rewards and recognition system and to broaden it at the departmental level such that it reflects the mission of the institution and the orientation of its faculty. At a time when faculty productivity is under critical examination, the academic community can ill afford to ignore the contributions from faculty who are perhaps less active in traditional areas of research but who have other skills and interests that do serve their institutions and the profession.

The first step in broadening and reforming the reward system must be a clear statement of the mission of the institution and its physics programs. The mission statement should be developed by the faculty in consultation with university leadership as well as with students, alumni, external review committees, and external advisory councils. Among the activities that might be included in the scope of a department's mission are:

1) To perform research in physics and related areas (including physics education), to secure extramural support for that research, to publish the results in peer-reviewed journals, to contribute to topical conferences, and to provide opportunities for students to participate in research

2) To recruit and educate talented undergraduate physics majors for diverse careers including (in addition to the physics profession) teaching, engineering, computer science, law, medicine, management, finance, and other careers in which analytical abilities are valued

3) To offer courses that provide the necessary physics background to students in all the basic and applied sciences

4) To offer stimulating general education physics courses to undergraduate students from diverse majors

5) To participate in the preparation of K–12 teachers

6) To recruit and educate graduate students in professional MS and PhD programs and prepare them for careers in academia, industry, or government services

7) To recruit students from underrepresented groups (women, minorities, students with disabilities) into undergraduate and graduate physics programs, and to conduct retention programs designed to maximize the success of all students in physics degree programs

8) To conduct outreach programs to disseminate knowledge about physics to diverse audiences, including K–12 students and teachers and the general public

Not all of these activities will be prominent in the missions of every department, and the weighting factors will certainly vary among departments. However, it is significant that the activities described in the mission statement must map onto the descriptions of faculty positions.

The physics community has begun to recognize the need to institute widespread reform of undergraduate and graduate education and to disseminate physics knowledge to diverse audiences. Yet paradoxically, we have been slower to offer reward and recognition to faculty who conduct these activities in a scholarly and professional manner. We support the broadening of the rewards and recognition system to include all activities that are recognized as part of a department's mission and that are undertaken in a manner consistent with other more generally recognized forms of scholarship such as basic or applied research. Success in these pursuits will require dedicated individuals, who must be provided with the motivation, resources, and rewards to make the necessary commitment of their professional energies. Just as the entire physics community has profited from the research done by talented individuals, so we will all profit from education and outreach done in a scholarly and professional manner. It is to the benefit of individual departments as well as to the general community to support and promote these activities with appropriate recognition.

Example 6

From *Scholarship in Psychology: A Paradigm for the 21st Century*

THE SOCIETY FOR THE TEACHING OF PSYCHOLOGY
AMERICAN PSYCHOLOGICAL ASSOCIATION
TASK FORCE IN DEFINING SCHOLARSHIP IN PSYCHOLOGY (1998)

A Five-Part Definition of Scholarship in Psychology

For most of the past 50 years, scholarship has been identified with original research that has been published in a peer-reviewed journal. Thinking of scholarship as contributions to the social fabric of psychology led us to a five-part definition in which any single dimension or any of the five parts in combination can be considered scholarship. We believe that applying this model when evaluating scholarship will result in a more meaningful use of faculty time and energy and that society, as a whole, will benefit. Readers may recognize the influence of Boyer's classic distinctions in these categories, although numerous changes have been made to his original conceptualization.

1) **Original research.** By original research, we mean the creation of new knowledge—collection of original data, an advancement in methods of inquiry, theory generation or testing, and the dissemination of this activity in a refereed scholarly journal or other outlet.

2) **Integration of knowledge.** New knowledge, represented in the category of original research, is of limited usefulness if it is not integrated into a larger body of concepts and facts. For this reason, the integration or synthesis of knowledge is as valuable and as difficult as the generation of original data. A quality synthesis will reveal new patterns of meaning and can advance the field by creating new knowledge based on the integrative framework. Review articles and books, meta-analyses, and well-crafted texts that bring diverse findings together to enhance knowledge are examples of scholarship involving the integration of knowledge.

3) **Application of knowledge.** Psychology is useful. We live this message when psychologists use their knowledge in applied settings. Applications can take many forms. They include writing amicus

briefs in which psychological evidence is used to assist judges in resolving difficult legal issues, developing software and other new forms of media in accord with our knowledge of how people think and learn, writing for a popular audience to help those with psychological problems, using psychological principles to establish or review community projects such as a school for learning disabled adults, and conducting site visits in which one's knowledge of a quality program guides the evaluation. These are examples in which society, at large, benefits from a faculty member's disciplinary knowledge.

4) **The scholarship of pedagogy.** This is one area of scholarship where psychology is different from other academic disciplines. Faculty in other disciplines teach, but psychology includes the science of pedagogy and thus should include research on teaching and learning at all levels (including prenatal learning and learning in infancy through old age), in all settings (in the home, on the job, at the market), and with all populations (persons with disabilities, the impoverished, the most gifted, nonhuman animals, and machine intelligence). Of course, the concern with issues of pedagogy also extends to instruction at the college level, where reflective scholars are concerned with questions about the extent to which we, as faculty in psychology, use our understanding of human cognition in our own teaching. When psychologists conduct research on ways to promote learning and evaluate the effectiveness of their applications, they are engaging in the scholarship of pedagogy. This is a question of scholarship and its application in the transfer of knowledge and in the creation of environments in which students learn.

5) **The scholarship of teaching in psychology.** Scholarship in teaching in one's subject area, like any of the other categories of scholarship, can vary in quality and in the extent to which it utilizes disciplinary knowledge. Teaching is scholarship when it makes an original contribution, for example, through synthesizing information in new ways or through an insight of psychological importance. Like all other forms of scholarship, it builds on an accumulated knowledge base. Teaching can be made public, and thus available for peer review, by assembling a teaching portfolio that might contain syllabi, student papers, tests, and statements of one's teaching philosophy and goals (Seldin, 1997). Peer visitation can also be used, with multiple visitors providing the degree of reliability that is needed

for valid assessment. Team teaching also provides an opportunity to make teaching public for peer review. Quality teaching that adheres to these criteria is substantive scholarship, and as such, it needs to be honored and rewarded. Everyone who teaches should aspire to the highest standards in this area of scholarship. Surely, if this assertion were taken seriously, we would have made a significant contribution to the betterment of society.

6

STUDENT RATINGS OF FACULTY: SPECIAL INSTRUCTIONAL SETTINGS (SELECTED EXAMPLES)

Laboratory

- To what extent did the assignments relate to course concepts?
- Were the laboratory activities coordinated with other work in the course?
- Was the instructor prepared for laboratory sessions and pre-activity discussions?
- Were you provided with adequate instructions for proceeding with your laboratory exercises?
- Did you have enough time in the laboratory to complete your exercises?

Studio

- Were you exposed to a variety of techniques and procedures?
- Did the instructor take time to work with you individually?
- Were the instructor's examples/demonstrations clear and concise?
- Did you have enough time to develop the skills you needed to succeed?
- Were the instructor's critiques of your work useful? Did you learn from them?

- Was the instructor sensitive to your problems?
- Did your instructor help you think about different ways to approach projects?

Team Teaching

- Did one instructor dominate the course?
- Were the faculty involved in teaching the course compatible with each other?
- Did the involvement of more than one faculty member provide you with insights that a single faculty could not?
- Was the instruction in the course coordinated?

Internship/Clinical

- Were you exposed to a variety of problems?
- Was the experience realistic?
- Were your questions thoroughly answered?
- Were problems clearly stated?
- Was evaluation consistent?
- Were appropriate and inappropriate clinical procedures/ approaches clearly identified and discussed?

These examples are based on items included in the Instructor and Course Evaluation System, Office of Instructional Resources, Measurement, and Research Division, University of Illinois at Urbana-Champaign.

7

Evaluating Teaching: Selected Additional References

Arreola, R. A. (2000). *Developing a comprehensive faculty evaluation system: A handbook for college faculty and administrators on designing and operating a comprehensive faculty evaluation system* (2nd ed.). Bolton, MA: Anker.

Braskamp, L. A., & Ory, J. C. (1994). *Assessing faculty work.* San Francisco, CA: Jossey-Bass.

Centra, J. A. (1979). *Determining faculty effectiveness.* San Francisco, CA: Jossey-Bass.

Centra, J. A. (1994). *Reflective faculty evaluation.* San Francisco, CA: Jossey-Bass.

Chism, N. V. N. (1999). *Peer review of teaching: A sourcebook.* Bolton, MA: Anker.

Davis, B. G. (1993). *Tools for teaching.* San Francisco, CA: Jossey-Bass.

Edgerton, R., Hutchings, P., & Quinlan, K. (1991). *The teaching portfolio: Capturing the scholarship in teaching.* Washington, DC: American Association for Higher Education.

Elman, S. E., & Smock, S. M. (1985). *Professional service and faculty rewards: Toward an Integrated Structure.* Washington, DC: National Association of State Universities and Land-Grant Colleges.

Hutchings, P. (1993). *Campus use of the teaching portfolio: Twenty-five profiles.* Washington, DC: American Association for Higher Education.

49

McKeachie, W. J. (1994). *Teaching tips: Strategies, research, and theory for college and university teachers* (9th ed.). Lexington, MA: D. C. Heath.

Office of Continuing Education and Public Service. (1993). *A faculty guide for relating public service to the promotion and tenure review process.* Urbana, IL: University of Illinois at Urbana-Champaign.

Rice, E. (1991). The new American scholar: Scholarship and the purposes of the university. *Metropolitan Universities Journal, 1* (4), 7–18.

Seagren, A. T., Creswell, J. T., & Wheeler, D. W. (1993). *The department chair: New roles, responsibilities and challenges.* ASHE-ERIC Higher Education Report No. 1. Washington, DC: The George Washington University, School of Education and Human Development.

Seldin, P. (1997). *The teaching portfolio: A practical guide to improved performance and promotion/tenure decisions* (2nd ed.). Bolton, MA: Anker.

Seldin, P., & Associates. (1999). *Changing practices in evaluating teaching: A practical guide to improved faculty performance and promotion/tenure decisions.* Bolton, MA: Anker.

Shulman, L. S. (1989, June). Toward a pedagogy of substance. *AAHE Bulletin, 41* (10), 8–13.

8

Evaluating an Advisor: Selected Items from the ACT Survey of Academic Advising

	DOES NOT APPLY	STRONGLY AGREE	AGREE	NEUTRAL	DISAGREE	STRONGLY DISAGREE
19. Allows sufficient time to discuss issues or problems.	O	O	O	O	O	O
20. Is willing to discuss personal problems.	O	O	O	O	O	O
21. Anticipates my needs.	O	O	O	O	O	O
22. Helps me select courses that match my interests and abilities.	O	O	O	O	O	O
23. Helps me to examine my needs, interests, and values.	O	O	O	O	O	O
24. Is familiar with my academic background.	O	O	O	O	O	O
25. Encourages me to talk about myself and my college experiences.	O	O	O	O	O	O
26. Encourages my interest in an academic discipline.	O	O	O	O	O	O
27. Encourages my involvement in extracurricular activities.	O	O	O	O	O	O
28. Helps me explore careers in my field of interest.	O	O	O	O	O	O
29. Is knowledgeable about courses outside my major area of study.	O	O	O	O	O	O
30. Seems to enjoy advising.	O	O	O	O	O	O
31. Is approachable and easy to talk to.	O	O	O	O	O	O
32. Shows concern for my personal growth and development.	O	O	O	O	O	O
33. Keeps personal information confidential.	O	O	O	O	O	O
34. Is flexible in helping me plan my academic program.	O	O	O	O	O	O
35. Has a sense of humor.	O	O	O	O	O	O
36. Is a helpful, effective advisor whom I would recommend to other students.	O	O	O	O	O	O

For information on the use of this instrument contact:
American College Testing Program
P.O. Box 168
Iowa City, IA 52243
(319) 337-1000

9

Documenting Effectiveness and Impact As a Member of a Team (Draft Statement)

To the Candidate

If you have been involved in a team project that you believe is an important element in your review, please include the following information.

- Title of the project
- Was the project funded by your institution or externally? If externally, who was the sponsor?
- If the project was undertaken with a specific charge to your team, what was the charge?
- Who were the other members of your team (address, phone and fax numbers, and email)?
- What were the specific problem(s) you were addressing as a team?
- What was your role on the team?
- What specific disciplinary expertise or other strengths did you bring to the project?
- Were there specific elements of the project in which you played a major role? What were they?
- Were you the (or a) primary author of specific materials? If so, what were they? Are they available for committee review?
- What was the impact of the project and how has it been determined?

Important: If this project is being presented as a major scholarly, professional, or creative activity, please describe the process that was followed and the results of the initiative. Impact and significance should be documented following the guidelines you have been provided.

10

ASSESSING COLLEGIALITY:
A FACULTY SURVEY

	Always	Usually	Some-times	Occasion-ally	Never
	5	4	3	2	1
1) Relationship with others					
a) Interacts with colleagues.	5	4	3	2	1
b) Interacts in a positive manner.	5	4	3	2	1
c) Engages in give and take of ideas and perspectives.	5	4	3	2	1
d) Treats others as professional equals by respecting their ideas, perspectives, and experiences.	5	4	3	2	1
2) Institutional citizen					
a) Takes his or her turn in doing some of the needed institutional/citizenship responsibilities.	5	4	3	2	1
b) Helps others understand the issues and possible solutions to improve the institution.	5	4	3	2	1

	Always	Usually	Some-times	Occasion-ally	Never
c) Uses his or her expertise to respond to institutional needs or problems.	5	4	3	2	1
d) Helps develop an environment of open exchange and willingness to help resolve institutional problems/issues.	5	4	3	2	1
e) Represents the institution in a professional manner— honest, factual, advocates for its functions, and projects a positive image.	5	4	3	2	1

	Very High	High	Average	Fair	Poor
3) Overall rating as a colleague	5	4	3	2	1

Developed by Daniel Wheeler, University of Nebraska

11

DOCUMENTING AND ASSESSING WORK OF FACULTY: SELECTED EXAMPLES

AUTHOR TEXTBOOK AS FUNDAMENTAL INTRODUCTION TO THE DISCIPLINE

Rationale

- Demonstrates high level of understanding of the field, ability to integrate knowledge, and ability to represent knowledge to others (and thus a teaching skill)

- May represent knowledge that is put together in creative or novel ways leading to new insights

- Integrates teaching and scholarly aspects of faculty role

- Has potential for leading to future scholarship

- Makes teaching public—cosmopolitan—beyond bounds of campus

- Helps other faculty think of different ways of organizing and presenting information

- May improve student learning and attitudes toward the discipline

Suggested Guidelines for Documentation

Evidence

- Descriptive essay—should include a statement of existing need, a discussion of how the text represents a new approach or paradigm, and the developmental process that was followed

- Product itself

- Reviews from publisher (during selection process)

- Published reviews

- Student assessments

- Sales (overall and by institution and type)

- Citations (where appropriate)

- Data on student learning and attitudes toward the discipline

- Enrollment in follow-up courses and programs

Criteria

- Marketability; fills important or unique niche; levels of adoption

- Quality, accuracy, clarity of content (peers)

- Presentation, style, learning impact (students)

- Impact on how subject is taught

- Degree of innovation (structure, content, and/or presentation)

- Epistemological impact; how knowledge is structured

- Student learning and attitudes toward the discipline improved

- Demonstrates scholarly process

DEVELOP A NEW HIGH SCHOOL CURRICULUM

Rationale
- Demonstrates the ability to communicate important concepts to a diverse population
- Can increase general student interest in the field
- Can prepare students for further study in the discipline
- Can represent a major new approach to education in the discipline
- Can improve student knowledge
- Can improve student's interest in the subject

Suggested Guidelines for Documentation

Evidence
- Descriptive essay—including statement of need, goals of the project, the design process that was followed, and the rationale for approach being used
- Reviews by experts in the field (college and secondary) and by teachers who are using the materials produced
- The materials
- Data on changes in student learning and attitudes
- Data on feasibility of continued and expanded use (cost, etc.)
- Data on student learning and attitudes
- Enrollment and attrition data

Criteria
- Represents a major innovation
- Quality and accuracy of content
- Meets specific needs of student population being served
- Has application beyond test site (adoption by other schools)
- Validated by an independent review process

- Met other needs that were identified (updating of context, correcting deficiencies, high failure rate, lack of interest in discipline, etc.)
- Demonstrates scholarly process

DIRECT A PLAY (STUDENT PRODUCTION)

Rationale
- Interpretation of the work involves research, creativity, and scholarship
- Requires disciplinary expertise and an historical frame of reference
- Requires the ability to make maximum use of existing resources (human and material)
- Provides theory/practice application for students in cast and serving in other production-related roles (teaching function)

Suggested Guidelines for Documentation
Evidence
- Descriptive essay—includes a statement of artistic, intellectual, and production goals; a description of the intellectual and/or production processes; and a rationale for the basic decisions that were made
- Videotape of final production for external peer review
- Critical reviews
- Students' evaluation and critique based on pre-established goals for learning (participants and audience)
- Increased student knowledge about the field, the author, and the social context in which she or he worked

Criteria
- Shows evidence of high level of disciplinary expertise
- Makes maximum use of existing resources
- Production is innovative, breaks new ground
- Demonstrates student learning (both participants and audience)
- Can be replicated
- Demonstrates scholarly process

DESIGN A NEW COURSE

Rationale
- Requires a high level of disciplinary expertise

- Can have major impact on student motivation, learning, retention, and attitudes toward the field of study. Can also increase interest of high quality students to major in field

- By improving learning, meets the stated goals of department, school, college, and institution

- Can help prepare students for other courses in the field and for successful careers

Suggested Guidelines for Documentation

Evidence
- Descriptive essay—includes statement of need and rationale for design, the process that was followed, and the rationale behind decisions that were made

- Syllabi or student manuals

- Newly created course materials

- Revised structure, change in role of faculty or students, appropriate applications of technology

- Video of class presentation (of innovative teaching strategies)

- Student ratings

- Student performance data (tests and test results). Focus, if appropriate, on specific population

- Comments regarding student preparation from faculty teaching high-level courses in the discipline

- Reviews of course and materials by experts in field (faculty and/or professionals)

- Results of field tests and revisions based on these data

- Comparative data on retention, class attendance, student attitudes, number of students selecting further study in the field

- Improved use of faculty and student time

Criteria

- Shows high level of disciplinary expertise
- Represents an innovation or new approach in design, delivery, or content that can be replicated
- Learning outcomes are clearly stated and match the course objectives
- Assessment measures stated outcomes
- Meets needs of student population being served and stated instructional goals
- Is approved by department and curriculum committee
- Improvements in retention
- Enrollment increases
- Demonstrates scholarly process

SERVE ON A COMMUNITY TASK FORCE APPOINTED BY CITY MAYOR

Rationale

- Requires high level of disciplinary expertise
- Can have major impact on reducing conflict within the community
- Fits within institutional mission statement regarding community service
- Can be used as a case study for classroom use or further research
- Can change attitudes of community leaders and the general public
- Can improve the quality of life in the community

Suggested Guidelines for Documentation

Evidence

- Reflective essay—describe problems being faced, role of the faculty member, and what faculty member learned or discovered and describes the process that was followed and the options that were selected
- Describes barriers that were encountered and how they were overcome
- Description of specific actions faculty member took as part of task force and reasons for those choices
- Transcripts or minutes of task force meetings
- Letters of commendation by task force chair or members focusing on the specific role played and his or her impact
- Written testimony from community groups who benefited from the work of the task force
- Course materials developed from this case
- Student interaction with faculty members' work or responses to case
- Institutional or unit goal statement articulating community service mission

- Committee interviews with key actors, mayor, community leaders, etc.
- Results of work of task force as evidence of impact on community (i.e., specific initiatives planned and accomplished)
- Publication and dissemination of reports

Criteria

- Demonstrates high level of professional expertise
- Demonstrates knowledge of recent research in conflict resolution
- Demonstrates strong performance as task force member
- Demonstrates innovative solutions to common societal problems
- Demonstrates sensitivity to various constituencies
- Interest in results, outcomes by other communities
- Publication of accounts of activity in news and other media
- Publication of accounts in disciplinary journals
- Changes in laws and policies
- Implementation of recommendations
- Demonstrates scholarly process

ASSIST A REGIONAL MUSEUM IN PRODUCING AN EXHIBIT ON INDIANS OF THE AMERICAN SOUTHWEST (HISTORIAN)

Rationale

- Requires a high level of disciplinary expertise
- Involves both original research and new conceptualization of the history and culture of the region
- Requires expertise in pedagogical theory and methodology
- Fits within the institutional mission of community service
- Fits within institutional mission to support cultural diversity

Suggested Guidelines for Documentation

Evidence

- Descriptive essay—describes problems being faced, the goals of the exhibit, its contributions to both research and teaching, and the design process that was followed
- Exhibit script and related publications
- Statement of educational goals and report on visitor evaluation
- Peer reviews of exhibit
- Data on learning improvements and attitude changes

Criteria

- Shows high level of disciplinary expertise
- Is innovative in conceptualization and presentation
- Is instructionally effective
- Approach can be applied by others
- Demonstrates ability to work effectively as a team member
- Demonstrates ability to be sensitive to educational level of intended audience
- Demonstrates scholarly process

DEVELOP A SOFTWARE SYSTEM TO MODEL STORM WATER RUN-OFF IN URBAN ENVIRONMENTS

Rationale

- Addresses a major environmental problem

- Demonstrates a higher level of disciplinary expertise

- Demonstrates a high level of competence in computer programming

- Demonstrates a high level of competence in environmental modeling

- By improving the design process, can reduce costs, improve decision making, improve safety, reduce flood damage

Suggested Guidelines for Documentation

Evidence

- Software package, including manual that details assumptions, limitations, etc.

- Descriptive essay—should describe problems being faced (i.e., statement of need), design rationale, benefits of the system, and what makes it an innovative approach

- Published reports and statements for users

- Data on applications (number of users and range of applications)

- Research data on impact (cost reductions in design, savings from reduced damage, etc.)

Criteria

- Marketability meets a defined need

- Quality of the system (external reviews)

- Adaptations and use of the system (national and international use)

- Impact of use (reduced costs, reduction in damage, etc.)

- Degree of innovation

- Demonstrates scholarly process

Documenting an Instructional Innovation or Use of Technology: Guidelines for Faculty

1) What was the specific problem you were addressing (unmet instructional goals, high drop-out or failure rate, reduced enrollment, attitudinal problems, poor attendance, poor participation in class, etc.)? Please document if data is available.

2) What specific innovations did you employ? What instructional materials or software did you use? What did you do differently?

3) Did you have any financial or professional support? (If so, what kind and from what source?) If you worked with other faculty what was your specific role?

4) Why did you do what you did? (Did you base your approach on reports, articles, research, etc.? If so what were they?)

5) What happened?

- Were your goals reached? What supportive data do you have?

- What did you learn? What worked, what didn't, and why?

- Did you have any unintended outcomes? (Did it take more or less of your time or your students' time than you expected? Were there any financial, space, or equipment surprises, etc.?)

6) Will you continue to use this approach?

- If so, will you do anything differently?

- If not, why not?

7) Will you be reporting what you did to others in your field? If so, how?

13

THE TEACHING PORTFOLIO:
NARRATIVE GUIDELINES FOR FACULTY

Your answers to questions posed on this worksheet will help form the basis of the narrative portions of your teaching portfolio. After you have gathered the relevant raw materials (see materials checklist), use this worksheet to make working notes. Describe your accomplishments and use details and examples where appropriate. Remember to be both selective and structured.

1) What are your teaching responsibilities? (Include your courses as well as any other teaching you do.)

2) How would you describe your teaching style and methods? Why do you teach as you do? Give examples and reasons.

3) What would you say your teaching strengths are? What are you most successful at and why? Examples?

4) How do you use course assignments, group work, email, or other tools to foster student learning? What is your emphasis in using these tools (e.g., integrating subject matter with students' experiences, motivating students to engage with the subject matter, giving students hands-on, active learning experiences)?

5) What have you done to become a more effective teacher?

   • List teaching workshops attended (topic, presenter, date, brief statement of impact on your teaching).

   • Informal classroom research you have conducted to evaluate and improve your teaching (e.g., one-minute papers, feedback cards, mid-semester evaluation, student journals, student evaluation teams). Be specific and include a statement of how the feedback affected your teaching).

- Your presentations, seminars, and publications on teaching in your discipline (list these as you do on your CV, annotating or providing details as necessary).

6) How do you stay current in the pedagogy of your discipline? How do you translate what you learn into your teaching?

7) What do others (colleagues, administrators, students, alumni, employers of graduates of your courses, etc.) say about your teaching?

Adapted from Seldin, P. (1997). *The Teaching Portfolio: A Practical Guide to Improved Performance and Promotion/Tenure Decisions* (2nd. ed.). Bolton, MA: Anker.

PROMOTION, TENURE, AND FACULTY REVIEW COMMITTEE CHECKLIST

Basic Information

☐ Review institutional, school/college, and departmental guidelines and policies (when candidate appointed and present)

☐ Review disciplinary/departmental statements describing the scholarly/professional/creative work of faculty

☐ Review letter of appointment

☐ Review specific assignments of candidate and supporting documentation

☐ Review procedures for documenting and evaluating the professional work of faculty including teaching, advising, and service

☐ Review requirements for scholarship

Information to Candidates

☐ The type of documentation the committee expects

☐ Suggested guidelines or structures of the portfolio and what to include

☐ The specific steps that will be followed

☐ The criteria that will be used to assess the quality of the materials provided

☐ Other resources (faculty, teaching centers)

The Review Process

General

- ☐ Are all required materials included?
- ☐ Will an external reviewer(s) be needed in candidate's area of disciplinary expertise?
- ☐ If institutional procedures and criteria have changed, which criteria will be used? Is the candidate aware of the standards he or she must meet?

Teaching

- ☐ Knowledge and uses of the research on teaching and learning
- ☐ Clearly stated learning outcomes with appropriate assessment procedures
- ☐ Effective and appropriate use of technology
- ☐ Appropriate mix of alternative learning strategies
- ☐ Good organization of subject matter and course
- ☐ Effective communication
- ☐ Knowledge of and enthusiasm for the subject matter and teaching
- ☐ Positive attitudes toward students
- ☐ Fairness in assessment and grading
- ☐ Flexibility in approaches to teaching

Advising

- ☐ Accessibility
- ☐ Quality of interchange
- ☐ Knowledge

Service, Non-Disciplinary (Citizenship)

- ☐ Range and significance of activities
- ☐ Quality of participation

Collegiality

☐ Relationship with colleagues and the institution

☐ Contribution to department and/or institution

☐ Meeting the needs of the institution

Scholarship (professional and creative work)

☐ High level of discipline-related expertise

☐ Breaks new ground or is innovative

☐ Can be replicated or elaborated

☐ Can be documented

☐ Can be peer-reviewed

Follow-up

☐ Procedure to support unsuccessful candidates

INDEX